D1474059

The Progress of Colored Women

Three Civil Rights Speeches by the First Black Woman to Receive a College Education in the United States of America

By Mary Church Terrell

Campaigner for Civil Rights and Suffrage and First President of the National Association of Colored Women

Published by Pantianos Classics

ISBN-13: 978-1987693775

First published in 1898

*Mary Church Terrell, painted c. 1940 by
Betsy Graves Reyneau*

Contents

Introduction

The address '*The Progress of Colored Women*' was delivered to the National American Women's Suffrage Association on February 18, 1898. Its charged and lucid passages represents the emergence of one of the most eloquent and convincing statements on life for black women. Describing the advancements which black women have made, and the great hurdles which still need to be overcome, the address tempers its triumphs with a recognition of the hardships wrought by the bigotry and oppression still ingrained in the minds of many in the United States'.

A pioneer in black rights, Mary Church Terrell was born in 1863, a daughter of two freed slaves. Demonstrating intellect from a young age, she sought a formal education. Mary's place as a lifelong campaigner and activist was cemented by her attainment of a Bachelor's Degree in Classics – she was the first black woman to ever attain a university degree. She went on to become the first President of the National Association of Colored Women, an organization which aims to advance the interest of black females in the USA. For decades she was a presence at rallies and events organized by campaigners for equal rights.

An eloquent and capable rhetorician and speaker, Mary personified the potential and capacity many black women strove for against the odds. Her life was spent tirelessly advancing her cause; marginalized on grounds of both race and gender, she became an authority on what such disadvantages ultimately lead to: the deprivation of countless capable, honest and worthy individuals of the life and attainments that they would otherwise enjoy, and the knock-on deprivation of a society which marginalized such people.

In the modern day, Terrell's speeches serve as historically valuable narrative of their time. More than fifty years after 'The Progress of

Colored Women' was delivered, the author remained an activist campaigning for an end to segregation in dining places. Happily, the author lived to witness the Supreme Court of the United States judge segregation in schools to be a violation of the Constitution.

This short book also contains two further addresses delivered by Terrell during her earlier years as an activist. *'In Union There is Strength'* stresses the need for solidarity and unity among black people, if the goal of equality in rights as citizens of the United States is to be attained. The second essay, *'What It Means to be Colored in Capital of the U.S.'*, notes several difficulties the author personally encountered and dealt with as a black woman living in the District of Columbia.

When she perished at the age of ninety in July 1954, Mary Church Terrell was lauded as an abiding and authentic link between the United States post-Emancipation, and the modern, post-war Civil Rights movement. Her legacy empowered black women to take leading roles in the fight for black rights, and energized the entire movement toward greater successes. Her oratorical legacy, whereby moving rhetoric is put to galvanizing purpose, would influence several of the civil rights movement's most successful campaigners.

The Progress of Colored Women

An address first delivered in 1898.

Fifty years ago a meeting such as this, planned, conducted and addressed by women would have been an impossibility. Less than forty years ago, few sane men would have predicted that either a slave or one of his descendants would in this century at least, address such an audience in the Nation's Capital at the invitation of women representing the highest, broadest, best type of womanhood, that can be found anywhere in the world.

Thus to me this semi-centennial of the National American Woman Suffrage Association is a double jubilee, rejoicing as I do, not only in the prospective enfranchisement of my sex but in the emancipation of my race. When Ernestine Rose, Lucretia Mott, Elizabeth Cady Stanton, Lucy Stone and Susan B. Anthony began that agitation by which colleges were opened to women and the numerous reforms inaugurated for the amelioration of their condition along all lines, their sisters who groaned in bondage had little reason to hope that these blessings would ever brighten their crushed and blighted lives, for during those days of oppression and despair, colored women were not only refused admittance to institutions of learning, but the law of the States in which the majority lived made it a crime to teach them to read. Not only could they possess no property, but even their bodies were not their own. Nothing, in short, that could degrade or brutalize the womanhood of the race was lacking in that system from which colored women then had little hope of escape. So gloomy were their prospects, so fatal the laws, so pernicious the customs, only fifty years ago.

But, from the day their fetters were broken and their minds released from the darkness of ignorance to which for more than two hundred years they had been doomed, from the day they could stand erect in the dignity of womanhood, no longer bond but free, till tonight, colored women have forged steadily ahead in the acquisition of knowledge and in the cultivation of those virtues which make for good. To use a thought of the illustrious Frederick Douglass, if judged by the depths from which they have come, rather than by the heights to which those blessed with centuries of opportunities have attained, colored women need not hang their heads in shame.

Consider if you will, the almost insurmountable obstacles which have confronted colored women in their efforts to educate and cultivate themselves since their emancipation, and I dare assert, not boastfully, but with pardonable pride, I hope, that the progress they have made and the work they have accomplished, will bear a favorable comparison at least with that of their more fortunate sisters, from the opportunity of acquiring knowledge and the means of self-culture have never been entirely withheld. For, not only are colored women with ambition and aspiration handicapped on account of their sex, but they are everywhere baffled and mocked on account of their race. Desperately and continuously they are forced to fight that opposition, born of a cruel, unreasonable prejudice which neither their merit nor their necessity seems able to subdue. Not only because they are women, but because they are colored women, are discouragement and disappointment meeting them at every turn.

Avocations opened and opportunities offered to their more favored sisters have been and are tonight closed and barred against them. While those of the dominant race have a variety of trades and pursuits from which they may choose, the woman through whose veins one drop of African blood is known to flow is limited to a pitiful few. So overcrowded are the avocations in which colored women may engage and so poor is the pay in consequence, that only the barest livelihood can be eked out by the rank and file. And yet, in spite of the opposition encountered, the obstacles opposed to their acquisition of knowledge and their accumulation of property, the progress made by colored women along these lines has never been surpassed by that of any people in the history of the world.

Though the slaves were liberated less than forty years ago, penniless, and ignorant, with neither shelter nor food, so great was their thirst for knowledge and so herculean were their efforts to secure it, that there are today hundreds of negroes, many of them women, who are graduates, some of them having taken degrees from the best institutions of the land. From Oberlin, that friend of the oppressed, Oberlin, my dear alma mater, whose name will always be loved and whose praise will ever be sung as the first college in the country which was just, broad and benevolent enough to open its doors to negroes and to women on an equal footing with men; from Wellesley and Vassar, from Cornell and Ann Arbor, from the best high schools throughout the North, East and West, Colored girls have been graduated with honors, and have thus forever settled the question of their capacity and worth.

But a few years ago in an examination in which a large number of young women and men competed for a scholarship, entitling the successful competitor to an entire course through the Chicago University, the only colored girl among them stood first and captured this great prize. And so, wherever colored girls have studied, their instructors bear testimony to their intelligence, diligence and success.

With this increase of wisdom there has sprung up in the hearts of colored women an ardent desire to do good in the world. No sooner had the favored few availed themselves of such advantages as they could secure than they hastened to dispense these blessings to the less fortunate of their race. With tireless energy and eager zeal, colored women have, since their emancipation, been continuously prosecuting the work of educating and elevating their race, as though upon themselves alone devolved the accomplishment of this great task.

Of the teachers engaged in instructing colored youth, it is perhaps no exaggeration to say that fully ninety per cent are women. In the back-woods, remote from the civilization and comforts of the city and town, on the plantations reeking with ignorance and vice, our colored women may be found battling with evils which such conditions always entail. Many a heroine, of whom the world will never hear, has thus sacrificed her life to her to her race, amid surroundings and in the face of privations which only martyrs can tolerate and bear. Shirking responsibility has never been a fault with which colored women might be truthfully charged. Indefatigably and conscientiously, in public work of all kinds they engage, that they may benefit and elevate their race.

The result of this labor has been prodigious indeed. By banding themselves together in the interest of education and morality, by adopting the most practical and useful means to this end, colored women have in thirty short years become a great power for good. Through the National Association of Colored Women, which was formed by the union of two large organizations in July, 1896, and which is now the only national body among colored women, much good has been done in the past, and more will be accomplished in the future, we hope. Believing that it is only through the home that a people can become really good and truly great, the National Association of Colored Women has entered that sacred domain.

Homes, more homes, better homes, purer homes is the text upon which our have been and will be preached. Through mothers' meetings, which are a special feature of the work planned by the Association, much useful information in everything pertaining to the home will be disseminated. We would have heart-to-heart talks with our women, that we may strike at the root of evils, many of which lie, alas, at the fireside. If the women of the dominant race with all the centuries of education, culture and refinement back of them, with all their wealth of opportunity ever present with them—if these women feel the need of a Mothers'

Congress that they may be enlightened as to the best methods of rearing children and conducting their homes, how much more do our women, from whom shackles have but yesterday fallen, need information on the same vital subjects? And so throughout the country we are working vigorously and conscientiously to establish Mothers' Congresses in every community in which our women may be found.

Under the direction of the Tuskegee, Alabama branch of the National Association, the work of bringing the light of knowledge and the gospel of cleanliness to their benighted sisters on the plantations has been conducted with signal success. Their efforts have thus far been confined to four estates, comprising thousand of acres of land, on which live hundreds of colored people, yet in the darkness of ignorance and the grip of sin, miles away from churches and schools. Under the evil influences of plantation owners, and through no fault of their own, the condition of the colored people is, in some sections to-day no better than it was at the close of the war. Feeling the great responsibility resting upon them, therefore, colored women, both in organizations under the National Association, and as individuals are working with might and main to afford their unfortunate sisters opportunities of civilization and education, which without them, they would be unable to secure.

By the Tuskegee club and many others all over the country, object lessons are given in the best way to sweep, dust, cook, wash and iron, together with other information concerning household affairs. Talks on social purity and the proper method of rearing children are made for the benefit of those mothers, who in many instances fall short of their duty, not because they are vicious and depraved, but because they are ignorant and poor. Against the one-room cabin so common in the rural settlements in the South, we have inaugurated a vigorous crusade. When families of eight eight or ten, consisting of men, women and children, are all huddled together in a single apartment, a condition of things found not only in the South, but among our poor all over the land, there is little hope of inculcating morality or modesty. And yet, in spite of these environments which are so destructive of virtue, and though the safeguards usually thrown around maidenly youth and innocence are in some sections withheld from colored girls, statistics compiled by men, not inclined to falsify in favor of my race, show that immorality among colored women is not so great as among women in countries like Austria, Italy, Germany, Sweden and France.

In New York City a mission has been established and is entirely supported by colored women under supervision of the New York City Board. It has in operation a kindergarten, classes in cooking and sewing, mothers' meetings, mens' meetings, a reading circle and a manual training school for boys. Much the same kind of work is done by the Colored Woman's League and the Ladies Auxiliary of this city, the Kansas City League of Missouri, the Woman's Era Club of Boston, the Woman's Loyal Union of New York, and other organizations representing almost every State in the Union.

The Phyllis Wheatley Club of New Orleans, another daughter of the National Association, has in two short years succeeded in establishing a Sanatorium and a Training School for nurses. The conditions which caused the colored women of New Orleans to choose this special field in which to operate are such as exist in many other sections of our land. From the city hospitals colored doctors are excluded altogether, not even being allowed to practice in the colored wards and colored patients—no matter how wealthy they are—are not received at all, unless they are willing to go into the charity wards. Thus the establishment of a Sanatorium answers a variety of purposes. It affords colored medical students an opportunity of gaining a practical knowledge of their profession, and it furnishes a well-equipped establishment for colored patients who do not care to go into the charity wards of the public hospitals.

The daily clinics have been a great blessing to the colored poor. In the operating department, supplied with all the modern appliances, two hundred operations have been performed, all of which have resulted successfully under the colored surgeon-in-chief. Of the eight nurses who have registered, one has already passed an examination before the State Medical Board of Louisiana, and is now practicing her profession. During the yellow fever epidemic in New Orleans last summer, there was a constant demand for Phyllis Wheatley nurses. By indefatigable energy and heroic sacrifice of both money and time, these noble women raised nearly one thousand dollars, with which to defray the expenses of the Sanatorium for the first eight months of its existence. They have recently succeeded in securing from the city of New Orleans an annual appropriation of two hundred and forty dollars, which they hope will soon be increased.

Dotted all over the country are charitable organizations for the aged, orphaned and poor, which have been established by colored women; just how many, it is difficult to state. Since there is such an imperative need of statistics, bearing on the progress, possessions, and prowess of colored women, the National Association has undertaken to secure this data of such value and importance to the race. Among the charitable institutions, either founded, conducted or supported by colored women, may be mentioned the Hale Infirmary of Montgomery, Alabama; the Carrie Steel Orphanage of Atlanta; the Reed Orphan Home of Covington; the Haines Industrial School of Augusta in the State of Georgia; a Home for the Aged of both races at New Bedford and St. Monica's Home of Boston in Massachusetts; Old Folks' Home of Memphis, Tenn; colored Orphan's Home, Lexington, Ky., together with others of which time forbids me to speak.

Mt. Meigs Institute is an excellent example of a work originated and carried into successful execution by a colored woman. The school was established for the benefit of colored people on the plantations in the black belt of Alabama, because of the 700,000 negroes living in that State,probably 90 per cent are outside of the cities; and Waugh was selected because in the township of Mt. Meigs, the population is practically all colored. Instruction given in this school is of the kind best suited to the needs of those people for whom it was established. Along with their scholastic training, girls are taught everything pertaining to the management of a home, while boys learn practical farming, carpentering, wheelwrighting, blacksmithing, and have some military training. Having started with almost nothing, only eight years ago, the trustees of the school now own nine acres of land, and five buildings, in which two thousand pupils have received instruction—all through the courage the industry and sacrifice of one good woman. The Chicago clubs and several others engage in rescue work among fallen women and tempted girls.

Questions affecting or legal status as a race are also constantly agitated by our women. In Louisiana and Tennessee, colored women have several times petitioned the legislatures of their respective States to repeal the obnoxious "Jim Crow Car" laws, nor will any stone be left unturned until this iniquitous and unjust enactment against respectable American citizens be forever wiped from the statutes of the South. Against the barbarous Convict Lease System of Georgia, of which negroes, especially the female prisoners, are the principal victims, colored women are waging a ceaseless war. By two lecturers, each of whom, under the Woman's Christian Temperance Union has been National Superintendent of work among colored people, the cause of temperance has for many years been eloquently espoused.

In business, colored women have had signal success. There is in Alabama a large milling and cotton business belonging to and controlled entirely by a colored woman who has sometimes as many as seventy-five men in her employ. In Halifax, Nova Scotia, the principal ice plant of the city is owned and managed by one of our women. In the professions we have dentists and doctors, whose practice is lucrative and large. Ever since the publication, in 1773, of a book entitled "Poems on Various Subjects, Religious and Moral," by Phyllis Wheatley, negro servant of Mr John Wheatley of Boston, colored women have from time to time given abundant evidence of literary ability. In sculpture we are represented by a woman upon whose chisel Italy has set her seal of approval; in painting, by Bougerean's pupil, whose work was exhibited in the last Paris Salon, and in Music by young women holding diplomas from the first conservatories in the land.

And, finally, as an organization of women nothing lies nearer the heart of the National Association than the children, many of whose lives, so sad and dark, we might brighten and bless. It is the kindergarten we need. Free kindergartens in every city and hamlet of this broad land we must have, if the children are to receive from us what it is our duty to give. Already during the past year kindergartens have been established and successfully maintained by several organizations, from which most encouraging reports have come. May their worthy example be emulated, till in no branch of the Association shall the children of the poor, at least, be deprived of the blessings which flow from the kindergarten alone.

The more unfavorable the environments of children, the more necessary is it that steps be taken to counteract baleful influences on innocent victims. How imperative is it then that as colored women, we inculcate correct principles and set good examples for our own youth, whose little feet will have so many thorny paths of prejudice temptation, and injustice to tread. The colored youth is vicious we are told, and statistics showing the multitudes of our boys and girls who crowd the penitentiaries and fill the jails appall and dishearten us. But side by side with these facts and figures of crime I would have presented and pictured the miserable hovels from which these youth criminals come.

Make a tour of the settlements of colored people, who in many cities are relegated to the most noisome sections permitted by the municipal government, and behold the mites of humanity who infest them. Here are our little ones, the future representatives of the race, fairly drinking in the pernicious example of their elders, coming in contact with nothing but ignorance and vice, till at the age of six, evil habits are formed which no amount of civilizing or Christianizing can ever completely break. Listen to the cry of our children. In imitation of the example set by the Great Teacher of men, who could not offer himself as a sacrifice, until he had made an eternal plea for the innocence and helplessness of childhood, colored women are everywhere reaching out after the waifs and strays, who without their aid may be doomed to lives of evil and shame. As an organization, the National Association of Colored Women feels that the establishment of kindergartens is the special mission which we are called to fulfill. So keenly alive are we to the necessity of rescuing our little ones, whose noble qualities are deadened and dwarfed by the very atmosphere which they breathe, that the officers of the Association are now trying to secure means by which to send out a kindergarten organizer, whose duty it shall be both to arouse the conscience of our women, and to establish kindergartens, wherever the means therefore can be secured.

And so, lifting as we climb, onward and upward we go, struggling and striving, and hoping that the buds and blossoms of our desires will burst into glorious fruition ere long. With courage, born of success achieved in the past, with a keen sense of the responsibility which we shall continue to assume, we look forward to a future large with promise and hope. Seeking no favors because of our color, nor patronage because of our needs, we knock at the bar of justice, asking an equal chance.

In Union There is Strength

First published in 1897.

In Union there is strength is a truism that has been acted upon by Jew and Gentile, by Greek and Barbarian, by all classes and conditions alike from the creation of the universe to the present day. It did not take long for men to learn that by combining their strength, a greater amount of work could be accomplished with less effort in a shorter time. Upon this principle of union, governments have been founded and states built. Our own republic teaches the same lesson. Force a single one of the states of the United States to stand alone, and it becomes insignificant, feeble, and a prey to the rapacity of every petty power seeking to enlarge its territory and increase its wealth. But form a republic of United States, and it becomes one of the great nations of the earth, strong in its might. Acting upon this principle of concentration and union have the colored women of the United States banded themselves together to fulfill a mission to which they feel peculiarly adapted and especially called. We have become National, because from the Atlantic to the Pacific, from Maine to the Gulf, we wish to set in motion influences that shall stop the ravages made by practices that sap our strength and preclude the possibility of advancement which under other circumstances could easily be made.

We call ourselves an Association to signify that we have joined hands one with the other to work together in a common cause. We proclaim to the world that the women of our race have become partners in the great firm of progress and reform. We denominate ourselves colored, not because we are narrow, and wish to lay special emphasis on the color of the skin, for which no one is responsible, which of itself is no proof of an individual's virtue nor of his vice, which neither is a stamp, neither of one's intelligence nor of ignorance, but we refer to the fact that this is an association of colored women, because our peculiar status in this country at the present time seems to demand that we stand by ourselves in the special work for which we have organized. For this reason it was thought best to invite the attention of the world to the fact that colored women feel their responsibility as a unit, and together have clasped hands to assume it. Special stress has been laid upon the fact that our association is composed of women, not because we wish to deny rights and privileges to out brothers in imitation of the example they have set for us so many years, but because the work which we hope to accomplish can be done better, by the mothers, wives, daughters, and sisters of our race than by the fathers, husbands, brothers, and sons. The crying need of our organization of colored women is questioned by no one conversant with our peculiar trials and perplexities, and acquainted with the almost insurmountable obstacles in our path to those attainments and acquisitions to which it is the right and privilege of every member of every race to aspire. It is not because we are discouraged at the progress made by our people that we have uttered the cry of alarm which has called together this band of earnest women assembled here tonight.

In the unprecedented advancement made by the Negro since his emancipation, we take great pride and extract therefore both courage and hope. From a condition of dense ignorance. But thirty years ago, we have advanced so far in the realm of knowledge and letters as to have produced scholars and authors of repute. Though penniless as a race a short while ago, we have among us today a few men of wealth and multitudes who own their homes and make comfortable livings. We therefore challenge any other race to present a record more creditable and show a progress more wonderful than that made by the ex slaves of the United States and that too in the face of prejudice, proscription, and persecution against which no other people has ever had to contend in the history of the world. And yet while rejoicing in our steady march, onward and upward, to the best and highest things of life, we are nevertheless painfully mindful of our weaknesses and defects [in] which we know the Negro is no worse than other races equally poor, equally ignorant, and equally oppressed, we would nevertheless see him lay aside the sins that do so easily beset him, and come forth clothed in all these attributes of mind and grace of character that claims the real man. To accomplish this end through the simplest, swiftest, surest methods, the colored women have organized themselves into this Association, whose power for good, let us hope, will be as enduring as it is unlimited.

Believing that it is only through the home that a people can become really good and truly great, the N.A.C.W shall enter that sacred domain to inculcate right principles of living and correct false views of life. Homes, more homes, purer homes, better homes, is the text upon which our sermons to the masses must be preached. So long s the majority of people call that place home in which the air is foul, the manners bad, and the morals worse, just so long is this so called home a menace to health, a breeder of vice, and the abode of crime. Not alone upon the inmates of these hovels are the awful consequences of their filth and immorality visited, but upon the heads of those who sit calmly by and make no effort to stem the tide of disease and vice will vengeance as surely fall.

The colored youth is vicious we are told, and statistics showing the multitudes of our boys and girls who fill the penitentiaries and crowd the jails appall and discourage us. Side by side with these facts and figures of crime, I would have presented and pictured the miserable hovels from which these youthful criminals come. Crowded into alleys, many of them the haunts of vice, few if any of them in a proper sanitary condition, most of them fatal to mental and moral growth, and destructive of healthful physical development as well, thousands of our children have a wretched heritage indeed. It is, therefore, into the home, sisters of the Association, that we must go, filled with all the zeal and charity which such a mission demands.

To the children of the race we owe, as women, a debt which can never be paid, until Herculean efforts are made to rescue them from evil and shame for which they are in no way responsible. Listen to the cry of the children, my sisters. Upon you they depend for the light of knowledge, and the blessing of a good example. As an organization of women, surely nothing can be nearer our hearts than the children, many of whose lives so sad and dark we might brighten and bless. It is kindergartens we need. Free kindergartens in every city and hamlet of this broad land we must have, if the children are to receive from us what it is our duty to give. The more unfavorable the environments of children, the more necessary is it that steps be taken to counteract the hateful influences upon innocent victims. How imperative is it then that we inculcate correct principles, and set good examples for our own youth whose little feet will have so many thorny paths of prejudice, temptations, and injustice to tread. Make a visit to the settlements of colored people who in many cities are relegated to the most noisome sections permitted by the municipal government, and behold the miles of inhumanity that infest them. Here are our little ones, the future representatives of the race, fairly drinking in the permissible example of their elders, coming in contact with nothing but ignorance and vice, till at the age of six evil habits are formed that no amount of civilizing and Christianizing can ever completely break. As long as the evil nature alone is encouraged to develop, while the higher, nobler qualities in little ones are dwarfed and deadened by the very atmosphere which they breathe, the negligent, pitiless public is responsible for the results and is partner of their crimes.

Let the women of the National Association see to it that the little strays of the alleys come in contact with intelligence and virtue, at least a few times a week, that the noble aspirations with which they are born may not be entirely throttled by the evil influences which these poor little ones are powerless to escape. The establishment of free kindergartens! You exclaim Where is the money coming from? How can we do it? This charity you advocate though beautiful in theory is nevertheless impossible of attainment. Let the women of the race once be thoroughly aroused to their duty to the children, let them be consumed with desire to save them from lives of degradation and shame, and the establishment of free kindergartens for the poor will become a living, breathing, saving reality at no distant day. What movement looking toward the reformation and regeneration of mankind was ever proposed that did not instantly assume formidable portions to the fainthearted. But how soon obstacles that have once appeared insuperable dwindle into nothingness, after the shoulder is put to the wheel and united effort determines to remove them! In every organization of the Association let committees be appointed whose special mission it will be to do for the little strays of the alleys what is not done by their mothers, who in many instances fall far short of their duty, not because they are vicious and depraved, but because they are ignorant and poor.

Through mother meetings which have been in the past year and will be in the future a special feature of the Association, much useful informatics in everything pertaining to the home will be disseminated. Object lessons in the best way to sweep, to dust, to cook and to wash should be given by women who have made a special study of the art and science of housekeep. How to clothe children neatly, how to make, and especially how to mend garments, how to manage their households economically, what food is the most nutritious and best for the money, how to ventilate as thoroughly as possible the dingy stuffy quarters which the majority are forced to inhabit... all these are subjects on which the women of the masses need more knowledge. Let us teach mothers of families how to save wisely. Let us have heart to heart talks with our women that we may strike at the root of evil. If the women of the dominant race with all the centuries of education. refinement, and culture back of them, with all their wealth of opportunity ever present with them, if these women felt a responsibility to call a Mother's Congress that they might be ever enlightened as to the best methods of rearing children and conducting their homes, how much more do the women of our race from whom the shackles of slavery have just fallen need information on the same subjects? Let us have Mother Congresses in every community in which our women can be counseled. The necessity of increasing the self respect of our children is important. Let the reckless, ill advised, and oftentimes brutal methods of punishing children be everywhere condemned Let us teach our mothers that by punishing children inhumanely, they destroy their pride, crush their spirit and convert them into hardened culprits whom it will be impossible later on to reach or touch in anyway at all.

More than any other race at present in this country, we should strive to implant feelings of self respect and pride in our children, whose spirits are crushed and whose hearts saddened enough by indignities from which as victims of unreasonable cruel prejudice it is impossible to shield them. Let it be the duty of every friend of the race to teach children who are humiliated on learning that they are descendants of slaves that the majority of races on the earth have at some time in their history been subjects to another. This knowledge of humiliation will be important when we are victims of racism. Let us not only preach, but practice race unity, race pride, reverence and sect for those capable of leading and advising us. Let the youth of the race impressed about the dignity of labor and inspired with a desire to work. Let us do nothing to handicap children in the desperate struggle for existence in which their unfortunate condition in this country forces them to engage. Let us purify the atmosphere of our homes till it becomes so sweet that those who dwell in them carry on a great work of reform. That we have no money to help the needy and poor, I reply, that having hearts, generous natures, willing feet, and helpful hands can without the token of a single penny work miracles in the name of humanity and right.

Money we need, money we must have to accomplish much which we ape to effect. But it is not by powerful armies and the outlays of vast fortunes that the greatest revolutions are wrought and the most enduring reforms inaugurated. It is by the silent, though powerful force of individual influences thrown on the side of right, it is by arduous persistence and effort keep those with whom we come in daily contact, to enlighten the heathen our door, to create wholesome public sentiment in the communities in hick we live, that the heaviest blows are struck for virtue and right. Let us not only preach, but practice race unity, race pride, reverence, and respect for those capable of leading and advising us. Let the youth of the race Be impressed about the dignity of labor and inspired with a desire to work. Let us do nothing to handicap children in the desperate struggle for existence in which their unfortunate condition in this country forces them to engage. Let us purify the atmosphere of our homes till it become so sweet it those who dwell in them will have a heritage more precious than silver or gold.

What It Means to be Colored in Capital of the U.S.

A Lecture Delivered in 1906.

Washington, D.C., has been called "The Colored Man's Paradise." Whether this sobriquet was given to the national capital in bitter irony by a member of the handicapped race, as he reviewed some of his own persecutions and rebuffs, or whether it was given immediately after the war by an ex-slaveholder who for the first time in his life saw colored people walking about like free men, minus the overseer and his whip, history saith not. It is certain that it would be difficult to find a worse misnomer for Washington than "The Colored Man's Paradise" if so prosaic a consideration as veracity is to determine the appropriateness of a name.

For fifteen years I have resided in Washington, and while it was far from being a paradise for colored people when I first touched these shores it has been doing its level best ever since to make conditions for us intolerable. As a colored woman I might enter Washington any night, a stranger in a strange land, and walk miles without finding a place to lay my head. Unless I happened to know colored people who live here or ran across a chance acquaintance who could recommend a colored boarding-house to me, I should be obliged to spend the entire night wandering about. Indians, Chinamen, Filipinos, Japanese and representatives of any other dark race can find hotel accommodations, if they can pay for them. The colored man alone is thrust out of the hotels of the national capital like a leper.

As a colored woman I may walk from the Capitol to the White House, ravenously hungry and abundantly supplied with money with which to purchase a meal, without finding a single restaurant in which I would be permitted to take a morsel of food, if it was patronized by white people, unless I were willing to sit behind a screen. As a colored woman I cannot visit the tomb of the Father of this country, which owes its very existence to the love of freedom in the human heart and which stands for equal opportunity to all, without being forced to sit in the Jim Crow section of an electric car which starts form the very heart of the city–midway between the Capital and the White House. If I refuse thus to be humiliated, I am cast into jail and forced to pay a fine for violating the Virginia laws....

As a colored woman I may enter more than one white church in Washington without receiving that welcome which as a human being I have the right to expect in the sanctuary of God....

Unless I am willing to engage in a few menial occupations, in which the pay for my services would be very poor, there is no way for me to earn an honest living, if I am not a trained nurse or a dressmaker or can secure a position as teacher in the public schools, which is exceedingly difficult to do. It matters not what my intellectual attainments may be or how great is the need of the services of a competent person, if I try to enter many of the numerous vocations in which my white sisters are allowed to engage, the door is shut in my face.

From one Washington theater I am excluded altogether. In the remainder certain seats are set aside for colored people, and it is almost impossible to secure others.... With the exception of the Catholic University, there is not a single white college in the national capitol to which colored people are admitted.... A few years ago the Columbian Law School admitted colored students, but in deference to the Southern white students the authorities have decided to exclude them altogether.

Some time ago a young woman who had already attracted some attention in the literary world by her volume of short stories answered an advertisement which appeared in a Washington newspaper, which called for the services of a skilled stenographer and expert typewriter....The applicants were requested to send specimens of their work and answer certain questions concerning their experience and their speed before they called in person. In reply to her application the young colored woman. . . received a letter from the firm stating that her references and experience were the most satisfactory that had been sent and requesting her to call. When she presented herself there was some doubt in the mind of the man to whom she was directed concerning her racial pedigree, so he asked her point-blank whether she was colored or white. When she confessed the truth the merchant expressed...deep regret that he could not avail himself of the services of so competent a person, but frankly admitted that employing a colored woman in his establishment in any except a menial position was simply out of the question....

Not only can colored women secure no employment in the Washington stores, department and otherwise, except as menials, and such positions, of course, are few, but even as customers they are not infrequently treated with discourtesy both by the clerks and the proprietor himself. . . .

Although white and colored teachers are under the same Board of Education and the system for the children of both races is said to be uniform, prejudice against the colored teachers in the public schools is manifested in a variety of ways. From 1870 to 1900 there was a colored superintendent at the head of the colored schools. During all that time the directors of the cooking, sewing, physical culture, manual training, music and art departments were colored people. Six years ago a change was inaugurated. The colored superintendent was

legislated out of office and the director-
ships, without a single exception, were
taken from colored teachers and given to
the whites....

Now, no matter how competent or su-
perior the colored teachers in our public
schools may be, they know that they can
never rise to the height of a directorship,
can never hope to be more than an assis-
tant and receive the meager salary therefore, unless the present regime is radi-
cally changed....

Strenuous efforts are being made to
run Jim Crow cars in the national capital.... Representative Heflin, of Alabama,
who introduced a bill providing for Jim
Crow street cars in the District of Columbia last winter, has just received a
letter from the president of the East
Brookland Citizens' Association "indors-
ing the movement for separate street
cars and sincerely hoping that you will

be successful in getting this enacted into a law as soon as possible." Brookland is a suburb of Washington.

The colored laborer's path to a decent livelihood is by no means smooth. Into some of the trades unions here he is admitted, while from others he is excluded altogether. By the union men this is denied, although I am personally acquainted with skilled workmen who tell me they are not admitted into the unions because they are colored. But even when they are allowed to join the unions they frequently derive little benefit, owing to certain tricks of the trade. When the word passes round that help is needed and colored laborers apply, they are often told by the union officials that they have secured all the men they needed, because the places are reserved for white men, until they have been provided with jobs, and colored men must remain idle, unless the supply of white men is too small....

And so I might go on citing instance after instance to show the variety of ways in which our people are sacrificed on the altar of prejudice in the Capital of the United States and how almost insurmountable are the obstacles which block his path to success....

It is impossible for any white person in the United States, no matter how sympathetic and broad, to realize what life would mean to him if his incentive to effort were suddenly snatched away. To the lack of incentive to effort, which is the awful shadow under which we live, may be traced the wreck and ruin of score of colored youth. And surely nowhere in the world do oppression and persecution based solely on the color of the skin appear more hateful and hideous than in the capital of the United

States, because the chasm between the principles upon which this Government was founded, in which it still professes to believe, and those which are daily practiced under the protection of the flag, yawn so wide and deep.

.

WITHDRAWN

CPSIA information can be obtained
at www.ICGtesting.com
Printed in the USA
LVHW041523100919
630593LV00010B/832/P

9 781987 693775